$ 7.50

Ethan Frome

Edith Wharton

D1039754

Abridged and adapted by Emily Hutchinson

Illustrated by James McConnell

A PACEMAKER CLASSIC

FEARON/JANUS/QUERCUS
Belmont, California

Simon & Schuster Supplementary Education Group

Golden Sierra
High School Library

Other Pacemaker Classics

The Adventures of Huckleberry Finn
The Adventures of Tom Sawyer
A Christmas Carol
Crime and Punishment
The Deerslayer
Dr. Jekyll and Mr. Hyde
Frankenstein
Great Expectations
Jane Eyre
The Jungle Book
The Last of the Mohicans
Moby Dick
The Moonstone
The Red Badge of Courage
Robinson Crusoe
The Scarlet Letter
A Tale of Two Cities
The Three Musketeers
The Time Machine
Treasure Island
20,000 Leagues Under the Sea
Two Years Before the Mast
Wuthering Heights

Copyright © 1991 by Fearon/Janus/Quercus, a division of
Simon & Schuster Supplementary Education Group,
500 Harbor Boulevard, Belmont, California 94002. All
rights reserved. No part of this book may be reproduced
by any means, transmitted, or translated into a machine
language without written permission from the publisher.

Library of Congress Catalog Card Number: 90-85001

ISBN 0–8224–9354–3

Printed in the United States of America

10 9 8 7 6 5 4 3

Contents

Prologue

I had the story, bit by bit, from various people. As usually happens in such cases, each time the story was different.

Several years ago, I spent some time in Starkfield, Massachusetts. It was then that I first saw Ethan Frome. He was the most striking figure in Starkfield, even though he was a ruin of a man. He was very tall. He had a careless powerful look that set him apart. He had a lameness that stopped each step like the jerk of a chain. His face was bleak and unwelcoming, and he looked like an old man. I was surprised to find out that he was only 52.

"He's looked that way ever since he had his smash-up. That was 24 years ago," said Harmon Gow. Harmon told me that the "smash-up" was what had caused the red gash across Ethan Frome's forehead. It had also shortened and warped his left side. Each step was difficult for Frome. Every day he drove from his farm to the post office at about noon. That was the same time that I went to the post office. So I saw him often. I couldn't help but notice that he seldom received anything but a newspaper. The only other mail he ever got was addressed to Mrs. Zenobia—or Mrs. Zeena—Frome. These envelopes came from companies that made medicine.

"It was a pretty bad smash-up?" I asked Harmon. I was thinking about how handsome Frome must have been. But now his strong shoulders were bent out of shape.

"The worst kind," said Harmon. "It would have killed most men. But the Fromes are tough. Ethan will probably live to be a hundred."

I took a look at Frome. I thought he looked half dead already. I told Harmon what I thought. Harmon replied, "I guess he's been in Starkfield too many winters. Most of the smart ones get away."

"Why didn't he?"

"Well, he had to care for his folks, then Zeena."

"And then the smash-up?"

"Yes," said Harmon. "He had to stay after that."

Harmon didn't seem to know or understand any more than that. I could sense that there was a lot more to the story. I'd soon learn what he meant when he said Frome had "been in Starkfield too many winters." In winter, the snow shut down the whole village. I began to see what life—or the lack of it—must have been in Frome's young manhood.

I was stuck in Starkfield because of a carpenters' strike that delayed my work there. That winter was the coldest one I ever spent anywhere. During my stay, I grew to understand why Harmon had said, "Most of the smart ones get away." I wondered what forces could have been strong enough to keep Ethan Frome from fleeing.

I was a boarder in the home of a widow known as Mrs. Ned Hale. Mrs. Hale's father had been the village lawyer. So her home was known as "lawyer Varnum's house." It was the largest house in the village. The Varnums were no longer wealthy, but Mrs. Hale did her best to keep up appearances.

In her "best parlor," I heard all sorts of gossip about the town. I heard this gossip from Mrs. Hale herself. I was hoping to hear more about Ethan Frome. But on this one subject she was fairly silent. She commented, "Yes, I knew them both . . . it was awful." That was the best she could do to satisfy my curiosity. So I went to Harmon Gow for more information.

All Harmon would say was this: "Ruth Varnum— you know her as Mrs. Hale—was always as nervous as a rat. She was the first one to see them after they were picked up. It happened right below her house, down at the bend in the road. They were all friends. I guess she just can't bear to talk about it. She's had troubles enough of her own."

Everyone in Starkfield had troubles enough of their own. The villagers seemed to agree that Ethan Frome's troubles had been greater than anyone else's. Yet no one could explain for me the look in Frome's face. Neither poverty nor physical suffering could have put such a look there. I might have been satisfied with the story I heard, except for one thing. That thing was the fact that I had personal contact with the man.

When I had arrived in Starkfield, I met Denis Eady, the rich Irish grocer. He had agreed to use his horses to take me to the train station every day. I had to take the train to get to my job. About the middle of the winter, Eady's horses fell ill of a local sickness. Most of the other horses in the village caught this same sickness. Harmon Gow told me that Ethan Frome's horse was still on his legs. Harmon thought that Frome would be happy to take me to the station. He knew that Frome could use the extra money.

I knew that Frome was poor. Still, I was surprised that he was so poor that he would want to do this. Harmon told me a few more things about the man. He said, "Even when Ethan could work hard on his farm, his parents ate up everything. I don't know how he manages now. First his father got soft in the head. Then his mother got sick and dragged along for years. And his wife Zeena—she always thinks she's sick even if she's not. Sickness and trouble: that's what Ethan's had on his plate, ever since the very first helping."

4

The next morning, I looked out the window and saw Ethan Frome. He was making room for me in his sleigh. For the next week, he drove me to the station in the morning. And he was there to pick me up every evening. It was only three miles, but the old horse was slow. Even with firm snow under the runners of the sleigh, it took nearly an hour each way. Frome drove in silence, holding the reins loosely in his left hand. He never looked at me. He never seemed to want a real conversation. He seemed to be part of the silent, sad landscape. Yet there was nothing unfriendly in his attitude.

I could sense that he felt totally alone. I didn't think it just because of his personal sorrow. I guessed that his sorrow was the result of too many Starkfield winters, as Harmon Gow had hinted.

Only twice did we get close to a conversation. One time I spoke of a job I'd had in Florida. I talked about the difference in climates. I was surprised to hear Frome say, "Yes, I was in Florida once. For a while, I could call up the sight of it during the winters here. But now it's all snowed under."

He said no more.

Another day, when I was getting on my train, I missed a book I had brought with me. I think it was about some recent discoveries in science. That evening, I saw the book in Frome's hand. "I found it after you were gone," he said.

I put the book into my pocket and thought no more about it. We traveled along in silence for a while. Then Frome turned his face toward mine.

"There are things in that book that I didn't know the first word about," he said.

I was surprised that he sounded sorry about this. I told him that I'd be happy to lend him the book.

He paused for a moment. Then he said, "Thank you—I'll take it."

I hoped that this would help us to communicate more easily. But something in his past history, or in his present way of living, had apparently worked to prevent this. At our next meeting, he said nothing about the book. We went back to our silences.

After about a week of this, one morning I looked out my window into a thick snowfall. The snow was very high. I was sure my train would be delayed. I had to be at my job for an hour or two that afternoon. I decided to try to get there—if Frome showed up. I don't know why I ever thought "if." I never really doubted that Frome would appear.

I knew him well enough not to act surprised when he showed up. I was surprised, however, when I saw where we were going. Frome was leading the horses away from the train station.

"Your train is blocked by another train that got stuck in the snow," he explained.

"But where are you taking me?" I asked.

"Straight to your job, the shortest way," he answered.

"In this storm? It's at least ten miles!" I exclaimed.

"This horse can do it, if you give him time. You said you had some business there this afternoon. I'll get you there." He said it very quietly.

I could only say, "You're doing me the biggest kind of a favor."

"That's all right," he replied.

Near the schoolhouse we took a road that led us past his sawmill. It seemed dead, with nothing working. Frome did not even look at it as we drove by. In silence we continued our ride. About a mile farther, we saw some starved apple trees. We also saw some fields lost under drifts of snow. Then we saw one of those lonely New England farmhouses that make the landscape seem even lonelier.

"That's my place," said Frome, with a jerk of his elbow. I did not know what to say. The snow had stopped, and the sunlight showed the house in all its unhappiness. A dying vine flapped from the porch. The thin wooden walls of the house seemed to shiver in the wind.

"The house was bigger in my father's time," Frome said. "I had to take down the 'L,' a while back."

I saw then the reason the house looked so strange. It was that the "L" had been removed. In many New England houses, an addition connects the main house to the woodshed and the cowbarn. This addition has storerooms and a tool house. This "L" shape seems to suggest a life linked with the soil. The storerooms and tool house suggest warmth and nourishment. Perhaps this is because the people who live there can get to their work without facing the weather. Thus the "L," rather than the house itself, seems to be the center of the farm. The fact that Frome's home had no "L" became for me a symbol of his own shrunken body.

As we passed his house, the snow began to fall again. It cut off our view of the house. When the snow started to fall, Frome stopped speaking. Our little sleigh moved along in silence, as usual. The wind, however, did not stop. It soon sprang up into a gale. The horse was as good as Frome had promised. We pushed closer to my job through the wild white scene.

In the afternoon, the storm let up, and I was able to get some work done. We soon set out for our trip back to Starkfield. We thought we had a good chance of getting there by supper. By sunset, however, the clouds gathered again. The winter night seemed to be coming upon us layer by layer.

The light of Frome's lantern was soon lost. Our sense of direction was disappearing as well. Finally we began to see some landmarks. But the old horse was starting to show signs that he was very tired. I began to blame myself for having accepted Frome's offer of a ride. I talked him into letting me get out of the sleigh to lead the horse. For about a mile or two, we struggled this way. Then Frome said, "That's my gate over there."

"Look here, Frome," I said. "There's no need for you to go any farther." I was thinking that I would walk the rest of the way.

Frome said, "You should not go any farther, either. There's been about enough of this for anybody."

I understood that he was offering me a place to stay for the night. Without answering, I turned into the gate. I followed him to the barn. There we unharnessed the tired horse. Then Frome unhooked the lantern and led me into the night, saying, "This way."

In the darkness, I almost fell into a deep snowdrift against the house. Frome went up the slippery steps of the porch. He dug a way for me through the snow with his boot. Then he lifted the lantern, found the latch, and led the way into the house. I followed him into a dark passage. We went toward the door of a room. Behind the door I heard a woman's voice complaining.

Frome stamped on the mat to shake the snow from his boots. Then he set his lantern on a kitchen chair, the only furniture in the hall. Finally he opened the door.

"Come in," he said. As he spoke, the complaining voice became quiet.

It was that night that I found the clue to Ethan Frome. And I began to put together this vision of his story.

1 Mattie at the Dance

The village lay under two feet of snow. The moon had set. Young Ethan Frome walked quickly along the deserted street. The night was perfectly still, and the air was dry and pure.

When he reached the end of the village, he stopped in front of the church. He looked up and down the street, but he could see nobody. The road below Lawyer Varnum's spruce trees was the most popular sledding place in the village. But tonight, not one sled could be seen. The silence of midnight lay on the village. All the life of the town was to be found behind the church windows. From those windows came the sounds of dance music.

The young man walked toward the basement door. He moved cautiously toward the nearest window. He held back so no one could see him. He peeked into a window.

Inside he saw many girls and young men. The music had stopped, and the musicians were eating pie and ice cream. The guests were getting ready to leave, and some were already getting their coats. Suddenly a young man with black hair shot into the middle of the floor. He clapped his hands. His signal took instant effect. The musicians took up their instruments, and the young man looked around for a moment. He found a young girl who had already wound a red scarf around her head. He led her up to the end of the floor. Then he whirled her to the tune of a Virginia reel.

Frome's heart was beating fast. He had been looking for the girl with the red scarf. He was annoyed that another eye had been quicker than his. The young man danced well, and his partner caught his fire. Frome saw her laughing and dancing.

The dancers were going faster and faster. The musicians, trying to keep up with them, played as if they were in a horse race. Yet it seemed to the young man at the window that the dance would never end. Now and then he turned his eyes from the girl's face to that of her partner. The partner's face had taken on the look of almost proud ownership.

Denis Eady was the son of Michael Eady, the successful Irish grocer. Until now, Ethan Frome had liked Denis Eady. But now he began to think Denis needed a horse-whipping. It was strange that the girl did not seem aware of it.

Frome usually walked into Starkfield to get his wife's cousin, Mattie Silver, on those evenings when she went out. It was his wife, Zenobia, who suggested that Mattie go out occasionally. Mattie had come from Stamford to help Zeena. Mattie did not receive any pay for her work. So Zeena thought it best that Mattie get out once in a while so she wouldn't feel deprived.

At first Frome resented having to go to the village to get Mattie. He worked long days on the farm, and he was too tired. But before long, he began to wish that he could pick her up every night.

Mattie Silver had lived under his roof for a year. He had liked her from the first day he met her. He soon came to know that he could show her things and tell her things. He could also see that she appreciated him and everything he told her.

During their night walks back home, he began to feel the strength of their attraction. He had always been more aware of natural beauty than the people around him. His earlier studies had made him more sensitive to the meaning of the universe. Before he knew Mattie, his emotions had stayed inside him. They were a silent ache, a pain that caused him great sadness. He did not think that anyone else felt as he did.

Then he learned that one other person felt the same way. At his side, living under his roof and eating his bread, was this person. He could say to her: "That's Orion down yonder. That big star to the right is Aldebaran. Those others—they are the

Pleiades." And there were other feelings that drew them together with a shock of silent joy. They both loved the cold red of sunset behind winter hills. They appreciated the sight of clouds and the shadows of trees on the snow. Once she said to him, "It looks just like a painting!" To Ethan, her words seemed to echo the words of his own soul.

As he stood in the darkness outside the church, he thought of these things. He watched Mattie whirl across the floor. He wondered how his dull talk could have ever interested her. The sight of Mattie being happy with others made him unhappy. He was glad that his wife had never shown any jealousy of Mattie. Lately, however, she had complained that Mattie was not a good housekeeper.

Zeena had always been "sickly." Frome had to admit that, if Zeena were really as sick as she acted, she needed help. Perhaps she needed more help than Mattie could give. Mattie had no real interest in housekeeping. She was quick to learn, but she was also forgetful and dreamy. She did not take her job seriously. At first Mattie was so bad at housekeeping that he couldn't help laughing at her. But Mattie laughed with him, and that made them better friends.

He tried to help her by getting up earlier than usual to light the kitchen fire. He carried in the wood for her. He helped her around the house during the day. He even crept down on Saturday nights to scrub the kitchen floor after the women had gone to bed. Zeena, one day, had surprised him when he was churning butter. She had turned away silently, with one of her odd looks.

Lately Zeena had shown that she was not happy with Mattie. One cold winter morning, she spoke from the bed behind him, as he was shaving.

"The doctor doesn't want me to be left with nobody to do for me." She said this in a whining voice.

He had thought she was asleep, so her voice surprised him. He looked toward her. He saw that her high-boned face looked gray against the white pillow.

"Nobody to do for you?" he repeated.

"If you say you can't afford a hired girl when Mattie goes."

Frome turned away, saying, "Why on earth should Mattie go?"

"Well, when she gets married, I mean," his wife said.

"Oh, she'd never leave us as long as you needed her," said Ethan.

"I wouldn't want to stand between Mattie and a smart fellow like Denis Eady," Zeena whined. "The doctor thought I should speak to you concerning a girl he's heard about. . . ."

Ethan laid down his razor and said, "Denis Eady! If that's all you're worried about, I guess there's no hurry to find another girl!"

"Well, I'd like to talk to you about it," said Zeena.

Ethan was getting dressed by this time. "All right. But I don't have time now. I'm already late."

Zeena lay watching him in silence as he dressed. But as he went toward the door, she spoke. "I guess you're always late, now that you shave every morning."

This statement scared Ethan more than any words about Denis Eady. It was a fact that since Mattie Silver had arrived, he had taken to shaving every day. His wife, however, always seemed to be asleep in the morning. He thought that she wouldn't notice any difference in his looks. Once or twice in the past he had observed something about Zenobia. She would let things happen without seeming to notice them. Then, weeks later, she would say, in a careless way, something that proved she had noticed all along.

Lately, however, he had not even been thinking about Zenobia. He had thought of little else but Mattie Silver. Now, as he stood outside the church, he saw Mattie spinning down the floor with Denis Eady. He began to feel nervous and worried, but he wasn't sure why.

2 Ethan Walks Mattie Home

As the dancers poured out of the hall, Frome hid in the darkness and watched them. Those who lived in the village began to walk home. Those who lived out in the country began to pack themselves into the sleighs that would take them home.

"Aren't you riding, Mattie?" a woman called. Ethan's heart gave a jump. Then he heard a clear voice answer, "Mercy no! Not on such a night."

She came out of the hall alone and stopped within a few yards of him. Because he was still hidden, she could not see him. She seemed to be wondering why he did not show himself. Then a man came up to her, and said, "No one's here to meet you? Say, Mattie, I've got my dad's sleigh. I knew I'd want to take a ride tonight. I'll drive you home. What do you say?"

The girl seemed to hesitate. Frome saw her twirl the end of her scarf around her fingers. Not for the world would he have let her know he was watching. It seemed to him that his life hung on her next move.

She stood perfectly still, watching Denis hitch up the horse to the sleigh. She let him lead out the

19

Golden Sierra
High School Library

horse, climb into the sleigh, and make room for her. Then, in a swift motion, she ran up the little slope toward the front of the church.

"Good-bye! Hope you'll have a lovely ride!" she called to him.

Denis laughed, and pulled the sleigh up next to her. "Come on! Get in quick! It's as slippery as thunder on this turn," he said. He reached out a hand to her.

She laughed back at him: "Good-night! I'm not getting in."

By this time they were so far away from Frome that he could not hear them. He saw Eady jump from the sleigh and go toward the girl. He tried to slip his arm through hers, but she skipped away. Frome's heart, which had swung out over a black void, trembled back to safety. A moment later he heard the jingle of Eady's sleigh bells as he pulled away. Then he saw Mattie walking back toward the church.

In the black shade of the Varnum spruce trees, he caught up with her. She turned with a quick "Oh!"

"Did you think I forgot you, Matt?" he asked.

She replied, "I thought maybe you couldn't come back for me. I knew Zeena wasn't feeling too good today."

"If you thought I hadn't come, why didn't you ride back with Denis Eady?"

"Why, where were you? How did you know? I never saw you!" Her wonder and laughter ran together like rivers in a spring thaw. He slipped an arm through hers. Neither of them moved. It was very dark under the spruces. He could barely see the shape of her head. He longed to rub his cheek against her scarf. He would have liked to stand with her all night in the blackness. She moved forward a step or two, toward the sloping road.

"Lots of people were coasting down the hill on sleds before the moon set," she said.

"Would you like to coast with them some night?" he asked.

"Oh, that would be lovely!"

"We'll come tomorrow if there's a moon," he said.

She pressed closer to his side. "Ned Hale and Ruth Varnum almost ran into the big elm at the bottom. We were all sure they were killed. Wouldn't it have been too awful? They're so happy!"

"Well, Ned doesn't steer too well," said Ethan. "You'll be safe with me!"

"That elm is dangerous, though. It ought to be cut down," she said.

They continued to walk, silently for a time. Finally, Ethan spoke up. "You'd have found me right off if you hadn't gone back to have that last dance with Denis." He could hardly pronounce the name without feeling the muscles in his throat stiffen.

"Why, Ethan, how could I tell you were there?"

"I suppose what folks say is true," he said, instead of answering her question.

"Why, what do folks say?" she asked.

"It's natural enough you should be leaving us," he answered.

"Is that what they say? Or do you mean that Zeena is not happy with me anymore?"

Their arms had slipped apart and they stood still. "I know I'm not as smart as I ought to be," she said. "There are lots of things a hired girl could do that I don't know how to do. I haven't got much strength in my arms. But if Zeena would only tell me, I would try. You should tell me what Zeena wants, Ethan. Unless you want me to go, too—"

Unless he wanted her to go, too! If only he could find the words to tell her how much he wanted her to stay. But all he could say was, "Come along."

They walked in silence through the blackness of the tree-shaded lane. The night was so still that they heard the frozen snow crackle under their feet. At last they got to Ethan's gate. The sense that their walk was over seemed to make Ethan speak up.

"Then you don't want to leave us, Matt?"

He had to lean down to catch her whisper: "Where would I go, if I did?"

The answer sent a pain through him. But her tone of voice filled him with joy. He forgot what else he had meant to say. He pressed her against him. They were so close that he seemed to feel her warmth in his veins.

"You're not crying, are you, Matt?" he asked.

"No, of course I'm not."

They turned in at the gate and walked past a low fence. Inside the fence were the Frome gravestones slanting at crazy angles through the snow. "We never got away—how should you?" they seemed to say to him. Whenever he went in or out of his gate he thought bitterly: "I shall just go on living here till I join them." But now all desire for change was gone. The sight of the little graveyard gave him a warm sense of security.

"I guess we'll never let you go, Matt," he whispered. He felt that even the dead, who were once lovers, must help him to keep her. He thought, "We'll always go on living here together. And some day she'll lie there beside me."

As they walked up the hill to the house, Mattie tripped. She grabbed his sleeve to steady herself. For the first time he stole his arm about her, and she did not resist. They walked on as if they were floating on a summer stream.

A dead cucumber vine dangled from the porch. It reminded Ethan of a black ribbon tied to a door for a death. "If it was there for Zeena—" he thought. Then he imagined his wife lying in their bedroom asleep. Her mouth would be slightly open, her false teeth in a glass by the bed.

Zeena usually left a key under the mat for them. He stooped down and felt for it. "It's not there!" he said, surprised. Such a thing had never happened before. A few minutes later, he heard a step on the stairs. Then the door opened and he saw his wife.

Against the darkness of the house, she stood up tall and angular. She held a quilt in one hand and a lamp in the other. The light, on a level with her chin, showed her wrinkled throat. It also deepened the hollows of her high-boned face under her curlers. Ethan felt as if he had never before known what his wife looked like.

"Guess you forgot about us, Zeena," Ethan joked.

"No. I just felt so mean I couldn't sleep."

Mattie came forward, the color of the red scarf in her fresh lips and cheeks. "I'm so sorry, Zeena! Isn't there anything I can do?"

"No, there's nothing." Zeena turned away from her. Then she walked out of the kitchen, pausing in the hall to raise the lamp. The gesture seemed to say that she would light their way up the stairs.

The doors of the two bedrooms faced each other across the hall. Tonight it seemed especially important to Ethan that Mattie not see him follow Zeena. "I think I'll stay down here and go over some papers," he said.

Zeena stared at him. The flame in the lamp cruelly brought out the lines in her face. "At this time of night? You'll catch your death. The fire's out long ago," she said.

Without answering, he moved away toward the kitchen. As he did so, he caught a warning glance from Mattie. Then Mattie began to climb the stairs ahead of Zeena.

"You're right, Zeena," he said. "It is powerful cold down here." With a lowered head, Ethan went up the stairs after his wife. He followed her through the door of their room.

3 Zeena Takes a Trip

There was some hauling of lumber to be done the next day. Ethan was out early. The winter morning was as clear as crystal. He loved the early morning stillness. It was when he was working outdoors that Ethan did his clearest thinking.

He and Zeena had not spoken a single word after the door of their room had closed on them. She had taken some medicine and wrapped her head in a piece of yellow flannel. Then she had lain down with her face turned away. Ethan undressed quickly and blew out the light. He did not want to see her when he got into bed. As he lay there, he could hear Mattie moving about in her room. Her candle cast a small ray of light under his door. He kept his eyes on the light until it went out. Then the room was perfectly black.

There was not a sound except for Zeena's sickly breathing. Ethan could think of only one thing—the warmth of Mattie's shoulder against his. Why had he not kissed her when he held her there? A few hours earlier he would not have dared to think of kissing her. But since then, he had seen her lips in the light of the lamp. Now he felt they were his.

In the bright morning air, he thought about Mattie. He had felt sorry for her because bad luck had brought her to them. Mattie Silver was the daughter of a cousin of Zenobia Frome. This cousin had married well and had taken over his father-in-law's pharmacy. But he spent more than the business earned. And he borrowed money from relatives. When he died, his wife found out just how poor they really were. The bad news hit her so hard that she died soon after hearing it. Mattie, at 20, was left alone. All she had was 50 dollars, which she got from the sale of her piano.

Mattie had a few talents. She could trim a hat, make molasses candy, recite a few poems, and play a few pieces on the piano. But none of these talents was enough to get her a job. Her relatives would not give her anything but advice. They had already given her father most of their savings. So they could hardly be expected to give any money to Mattie.

Then Zenobia's doctor said that she should have some help around the house. The relatives saw a chance of getting some payment out of Mattie for their lost savings. Zenobia did not think Mattie could do much, but she decided to use her anyway. Zenobia loved to find fault with people, and she knew she could do that with Mattie. And so Mattie came to Starkfield.

Even though Zenobia was hard to please, Mattie

did her best. Ethan could at least pretend that he had a peaceful home. Since the previous night, however, Ethan was starting to feel a sense of dread. When his morning work was done, he trudged back home through the fields. As he entered the kitchen, he saw Zeena sitting at the table. He stopped short at the sight of her. Instead of her usual clothing, she wore her best dress and a bonnet. On the floor was his old suitcase.

"Why, where are you going, Zeena?" he exclaimed.

"I've got my shooting pains so bad that I'm going over to Bettsbridge to see that new doctor. I'll be staying with Aunt Martha Pierce for one night." She announced this in a very ordinary tone of voice. It was the same tone she used to say she was going to the basement to look at the preserves.

Zeena had done such things before. Ethan had grown to dread these trips of hers because of their cost. Zeena always came back with expensive medicine. This time, though, he felt a sense of relief. He now believed that she had been telling the truth the night before. He thought she really had sat up because she felt "too mean" to sleep. As usual, she seemed to be totally concerned with her own health.

Ethan did some quick thinking. He knew that during the winter months there was no stage between Starkfield and Bettsbridge. The trains were

slow and did not come often. Ethan knew that Zeena could not be back at the farm before the next evening. . . .

It was arranged that Jotham, Ethan's hired hand, would drive Zeena to the station. As they spoke about this, Ethan noticed how old Zeena looked. The light from the window made her face look especially drawn and bloodless. It sharpened the wrinkles between her ears and cheeks. It exaggerated the thin lines from her nose to the corners of her mouth. She was only seven years older than Ethan. Although Ethan was only 28, Zeena was already an old woman.

Ethan could think of only one thing. For the first time since Mattie had come, Zeena would be away for a night. He wondered if Mattie were thinking of it, too.

He thought that Zeena might wonder why he wasn't going to drive her to the station. Without really thinking, he said, "I'd take you myself, but I've got to collect cash for the lumber."

As soon as he said this, he was sorry. If Zeena thought he would be getting money, she would spend more on medicine. Zeena's only reply was to take the last bit of medicine from a bottle that was on the table. "This medicine hasn't done me any good, but I might as well use it up," she said. Then she pushed the empty bottle toward Mattie. "If you can get the taste out, you can use it for pickles."

4 An Evening Together

Right after his wife left, Ethan took his coat and cap from the peg. Mattie was washing the dishes, humming one of the dance tunes of the night before. He said, "So long, Matt." She answered, "So long, Ethan," and that was all.

It was warm and bright in the kitchen. The sun slanted through the window, and the cat dozed in the chair. The geraniums on the windowsill made the room seem even more cheerful. Ethan would have liked to stay there and just watch Mattie tidy up. It was more important, though, to get the hauling done. Ethan wanted to be back at the farm before night.

All the way to the village he thought of his return to Mattie. The kitchen was rather rundown, but it was surprising how homey it seemed with Zeena gone. He pictured what it would be like that evening. He and Mattie would be alone together indoors for the first time. They would sit there like a married couple. He would be in his stocking feet and smoking his pipe. She would be laughing and talking in the funny way she had.

The sweetness of this picture made him so happy

that he whistled and sang aloud. He still had a spark of friendliness in him, one that the cold Starkfield winters had not put out. Although his nature was serious and quiet, he really enjoyed friendly human contact.

As the years had passed, however, he spent more and more time alone. After his father's accident, he had to take care of the farm. Then, when his mother fell ill, she hardly ever talked. His cousin Zenobia Pierce had then come over from the next valley to help. Because the house had been so silent for so long, Zeena's voice was music to Ethan's ears.

Then Ethan's mother had died. After the funeral, when Ethan saw Zeena preparing to go away, he was seized with dread. The thought of being left alone was more than he could take. Before he knew what he was doing, he had asked her to stay. Since then, he had often thought that it wouldn't have happened if his mother had died in spring instead of winter.

When they married, they agreed to sell the farm and go to a large town. Ethan had always wanted to be an engineer. He dreamed of towns where there were lectures and big libraries. He wanted to live where there were "fellows doing things." He'd had a minor engineering job in Florida some time before. He felt sure that he could make his place in the world.

Unfortunately, no buyers came to the farm. While he waited for someone to buy, Ethan realized that it would be impossible to move Zeena. She chose to look down on Starkfield. Ethan knew that she could not live in a place that looked down on her.

Within a year of their marriage, she developed the "sickliness" that she was known for in their community. When she had first come to take care of his mother, Ethan thought Zeena was a wonderful nurse. Now he could see that her nursing skill was the result of her attention to her own symptoms.

Then she, too, fell silent. She said it was because Ethan "never listened." This had some truth to it. When she spoke it was only to complain. She complained of things not in his power to change. Finally he began to think of other things while she talked. Lately he began to think that she used her silence to hide her resentments. This feeling was very strong the night before, when he had seen her standing at the kitchen door.

Now that she had gone to Bettsbridge, he felt better. All his thoughts were on spending the evening with Mattie. Only one thing bothered him. That was his telling Zeena that he would get cash for the lumber.

When Ethan drove into Hale's yard, the builder was just getting out of his sleigh. Hale's large family kept him "behind" in most of his payments. Ethan did not like his chances, but he finally managed to ask for an advance of 50 dollars.

The blood rushed to his thin skin when he saw how astonished Hale was. It was Hale's custom to pay at the end of three months. Ethan had never asked for the money any sooner than that.

Ethan thought that if he'd said he really needed the money, Hale would have paid. Ethan was too proud to do this, however. He did not want Hale, or anyone else, to think he was desperate.

Hale refused in a good-natured way. He treated the matter like a practical joke. He asked if Ethan was going to buy a grand piano or build an addition to his house.

After an embarrassed pause, Ethan wished Hale good day and started to leave. As he did so, Hale suddenly asked, "See here—you're not in a tight place, are you?"

"Not a bit," said Ethan, keeping his pride.

"Well, that's good! Because I am, in fact. The truth is that I was going to ask for a little extra time on this payment. Business is slow, and money is pretty tight for me right now."

Ethan left his horses in Hale's stable and went into the village to do a few things. The afternoon was drawing to an end. The bitter weather had driven everyone indoors. Ethan had the street to himself. Suddenly he heard sleigh-bells, and a sleigh passed by him. Ethan recognized Denis Eady, in a handsome new fur cap. Eady leaned forward and waved a greeting. "Hello, Ethe!" he shouted and spun on.

The sleigh was going in the direction of the Frome farm. Ethan's heart skipped a beat. He thought Denis Eady had heard that Zeena had left. Maybe he was on his way to spend an hour with Mattie! Ethan was ashamed of himself for being so jealous.

After he was done in the village, he went back to Hale's stable. He got his horses and started back to his farm. As he got close to home, he saw a light in the house. "She's up in her room, fixing herself up for supper," he thought. He remembered how Zeena had stared at Mattie on her first night with them. Mattie had come down to supper with smoothed hair and a ribbon at her neck.

He opened the barn door, half-fearing to see Denis Eady's horse inside. Then he whistled cheerfully as he saw that his old horse was there alone. When he reached the kitchen door, he turned the handle. He was surprised to find that the door was locked. Then he realized that Mattie was alone. It was natural that she would lock the door.

In a minute or two he saw a line of light around the door, just as he'd seen it the night before. He half expected to see Zeena open the door. But when it did open, Mattie faced him.

She stood just as Zeena had stood, holding a lifted lamp in her hand. She held the light at the same level, and it brought out the beauty of her slim young throat. It also brought out the color of her lips, and edged her eyes with a velvet shade.

She had put a red ribbon in her hair. Ethan thought she seemed taller and fuller, more womanly in shape and motion. She stood aside, smiling silently, while he entered the kitchen. When she set the lamp on the table, he saw that it was set for supper. She had put out fresh doughnuts and stewed blueberries. In addition, she had put his favorite pickles in a red glass dish. A bright fire glowed in the stove and the cat lay stretched before it comfortably.

Ethan felt a sense of well-being. He went into the hall to hang up his coat and pull off his wet boots. When he came back, Mattie had set the teapot on the table.

"Well, Matt, any visitors?" he asked, as casually as he could.

She nodded and laughed. "Yes, one," she said, and he felt a blackness settling on his brows.

"Who was that?" he asked.

Her eyes danced. "Why, it was Jotham Powell. He came in after he got back from the station. He asked for some coffee before he went back home."

37

Golden Sierra
High School Library

The blackness lifted, and light flooded Ethan's brain. "Was that all? Well, I hope you gave him some." After a pause he added, "I suppose he got Zeena to the station?"

"Oh, yes, in plenty of time."

The name threw a chill between them. Suddenly Mattie said with a shy laugh, "I guess it's about time for supper."

They drew their seats up to the table. The cat jumped between them into Zeena's empty chair. They both laughed.

A moment earlier, Ethan had felt himself ready to speak to Mattie of important and wonderful things. The mention of Zeena had changed all that. Mattie seemed to have caught Ethan's embarrassment. She sat with her eyes cast down. Ethan pretended to be extremely interested in the doughnuts and sweet pickles. At last, he took a long gulp of tea and cleared his throat. He said, "Looks as if there will be more snow."

She acted as if this were really interesting. "Is that so? Do you suppose it will hold Zeena up?" She flushed red as the question escaped her. She quickly set down the cup she was holding.

Ethan reached over for another helping of pickles. "You never can tell, this time of year." The name had come up again. Once more he felt as if Zeena were in the room between them.

The cat, meanwhile, had crept up to the table and was heading toward the milk jug. Ethan and Mattie leaned forward at the same moment. Their hands met on the handle of the jug. Ethan kept his hand on hers a moment longer than necessary. The cat backed up, right into the pickle dish. The dish fell to the floor with a crash.

In an instant, Mattie sprang up from her chair. She went down on her knees by the pieces of glass.

"Oh, Ethan, Ethan—it's all in pieces! What will Zeena say?"

By now his courage was up. "Well, she'll have to say it to the cat, anyway!" he laughed. He knelt down by Mattie's side to scrape up the swimming pickles.

She lifted her eyes to him. "Yes, but, you see, she never meant for it to be used. She never even used this dish for company. I had to use the ladder to get it from the top shelf of the china closet. Of course, she'll want to know why I did it—"

It was more serious than Ethan had known.

"She doesn't have to find out," he said. "I'll get another one just like it tomorrow. Where did it come from? I'll go to Shadd's Falls for it if I have to!"

"Oh, you'll never get another even there! It was a wedding present—don't you remember? It came all the way from Philadelphia, from Zeena's aunt. That's why she wouldn't ever use it. Oh, Ethan, Ethan, what in the world shall I do?"

She began to cry. He felt as if every one of her tears were pouring over him like burning lead. "Don't, Matt, don't—oh, don't!" he begged her.

She got to her feet and carried the pieces of glass to the kitchen counter. It seemed to him as if the shattered pieces of their evening lay there.

"Here, give them to me," he said.

"Oh, Ethan, what are you going to do?"

Without answering her, he took the pieces into his broad palm. He walked out of the kitchen to the hall, where the china closet was. He reached to the highest shelf and laid the pieces there. From below, no one could tell that the dish was broken. He would glue it together the next morning. Months might pass before Zeena would notice. In the meantime, he might be able to find another one. He went back to the kitchen with a lighter step. Mattie was cleaning the last bits of pickle from the floor.

"It's all right, Matt. Come back and finish supper," he said.

She smiled at him through tear-hung lashes. His soul swelled with pride as he saw that he had comforted her. She did not even ask what he had done. Except when steering a big log down the mountain, he had never felt so much in control.

5 After Supper

They finished supper. While Mattie cleared the table, Ethan went to look at the cows. The earth lay dark and the air was very still. When he returned to the kitchen, Mattie had pushed up his chair to the stove. She had seated herself next to the lamp with a bit of sewing. The scene was just as Ethan had dreamed of it that morning. He sat down, pulled out his pipe, and stretched his feet to the glow. He had a confused sense of being in another world. The only drawback to his complete well-being was that he could not see Mattie from where he sat. He said, "Come over here and sit by the stove."

Mattie went over to sit in Zeena's empty rocking chair. Perhaps the reason Mattie felt uncomfortable was that it was Zeena's chair. After a moment, she got to her feet, saying, "I can't see to sew." She went back to her chair by the lamp.

Ethan got up, pretending to feed the fire in the stove. When he returned to his seat, he pushed it a little so that he could get a view of Mattie. The cat, who had been watching these unusual movements, jumped up into Zeena's chair. It lay watching them with narrowed eyes.

Deep quiet sank on the room. The clock ticked, and now and then a piece of wood fell in the stove. The faint sharp scent of the geraniums mixed with Ethan's smoke.

Soon the two began to talk easily and simply. They spoke of everyday things, like the weather, the next church social, the loves and quarrels of Starkfield. Ethan began to imagine that they had always spent their evenings this way and would always go on doing so.

"This is the night we were to have gone coasting, Matt." He said it as if they could go on any other night they chose, since they had all time before them.

She smiled back at him. "I guess you forgot!"

"No, I didn't forget. But it's as dark as coal outdoors. We might go tomorrow if there's a moon."

She laughed with pleasure. "That would be lovely, Ethan!"

He kept his eyes on her, marvelling at the way her face changed as they talked. "Would you be scared to go coasting with me on a night like this?" he asked.

Her cheeks burned redder. "I'm not any more scared than you are!"

"Well, I'd be scared, then. I wouldn't do it. That's an ugly corner down by the big elm. If a fellow didn't keep his eyes open, he'd crash into it." He felt as if he were protecting her. "I guess we're well enough here."

She let her lids sink slowly, in the way he loved. "Yes, we're well enough here," she sighed.

A few moments passed. Ethan said, "I suppose Ruth Varnum and Ned Hale will be setting a wedding date before long."

"Yes. I wouldn't be surprised if they got married some time in the summer." She said the word *married* as if her voice caressed it.

A pang shot through Ethan, and he said, "It'll be your turn next, I guess."

She laughed a little uncertainly. "Why do you keep on saying that?"

"I guess so I can get used to the idea."

He watched her hands as she continued to sew. Then she said, without looking up, "It's not because you think Zeena has something against me, is it?"

"Why, what do you mean?" he stammered, dread rising in him.

She raised her eyes to his. "I don't know. I thought last night she seemed to have."

"I'd like to know what," he growled.

"Nobody can tell with Zeena." It was the first time they had ever spoken about her attitude toward Mattie. "She hasn't said anything to you?" asked Mattie.

44

He shook his head. "No, not a word."

She tossed her hair back with a laugh. "I guess I'm just nervous, then. I'm not going to think about it anymore."

"Oh, no—let's not think about it, Matt!"

She sat silent, her hands busy with her work. It seemed to him that a warm current flowed from her toward him. Cautiously he slid his hand along the table. His fingers touched the material she was working on. A faint movement of her lashes seemed to show that she noticed. She let her hands lie still on the other side of the material.

Suddenly the cat darted from Zeena's chair. This made the empty chair rock by itself.

"She'll be rocking in it herself this time tomorrow," Ethan thought. "I've been in a dream, and this is the only evening we'll ever have together." The return to reality was very painful.

His change of mood affected Mattie, too. She looked at him, and her glance fell on his hand. He was still touching the material as if it were Mattie herself. Without knowing what he did, he bent over and kissed the fabric he was holding. As his lips rested on it, he felt that Mattie had risen. She was putting her work away.

He stood up also. The clock struck eleven.

"Is the fire all right?" she asked in a low voice.

As he checked the fire, she dragged over the box

the cat used for a bed. She put it near the stove. Then she lifted the geranium pots and moved them away from the cold window. He followed her and carried some of the other house plants away from the window.

When these nightly duties were done, there was nothing to do but light the candle and blow out the lamp. Ethan handed the candlestick to Mattie, and she went out of the kitchen.

"Good night, Matt," he said as she put her foot on the first step of the stairs.

She turned and looked at him a moment. "Good night, Ethan." Then she went up.

A moment later, the door of her room closed. He remembered that he had not even touched her hand.

6 Zeena Returns

The next morning at breakfast Jotham Powell was between them. Ethan tried to hide his joy by throwing scraps to the cat and complaining about the weather. He didn't even offer to help Mattie when she cleared the dishes.

He didn't know why he was so happy. Nothing was changed in his life or hers. He had not even touched the tip of her finger or looked her full in the eyes. But their evening together had shown him what life at her side would be like.

There was a load of lumber to be hauled to the village. Jotham Powell had come around to help load it. Ethan planned to have Jotham pick up Zeena. At the same time, Ethan would be delivering the lumber.

Jotham went out to harness the horses. For a moment Ethan and Mattie had the kitchen to themselves. She had plunged the breakfast dishes into a dishpan. The steam from the water caused her hair to curl into little brown rings.

Ethan stood looking at her, his heart in his throat. He wanted to say, "We shall never be alone again like this." Instead, he said, "I guess I can be home in time for dinner."

She answered, "All right, Ethan." He heard her singing over the dishes as he went.

Ethan planned to go to the village right after the lumber was loaded. He was going to buy the glue for the pickle dish. With ordinary luck, he should have had time to carry out this plan. But everything went wrong from the start.

One of the horses slipped on some ice and cut his knee. Then, because of a sleety rain, the lumber was slippery. It took twice as long as usual to load it. Then, instead of going to the village, Ethan had to lead the injured horse home. He wanted to wash the cut himself.

By the time he got going, Ethan had hardly enough time to carry out his plan. If the roads were good and the train late, he would make it back before Zeena got there.

He worked like ten men at unloading the lumber. Then he hurried over to Michael Eady's store for the glue. Denis Eady said they were sold out, and Ethan had to go to Mrs. Homan's store. Finally, she found one little bottle of glue, hiding among the cough drops.

"I hope Zeena hasn't broken anything she really likes," she called after Ethan as he left.

The barn was empty when he got home. After getting the horses settled, he walked up to the house and pushed open the kitchen door.

Mattie was there alone, as he had pictured her. She was bending over a pan on the stove. At the sound of his step, she turned with a start. She sprang over to him.

"See here, Matt, I've got some stuff to mend the dish with. Let me get at it quick," he cried, waving the bottle in one hand. She did not seem to hear him.

"Oh, Ethan—Zeena's come," she said in a whisper, clutching his sleeve.

They stood and stared at each other. "But the sleigh is not in the barn!" Ethan stammered.

"Jotham brought some things back for his wife, and he drove right on home. He'll return the sleigh later," she explained.

"How is she?" he asked, dropping his voice to Mattie's whisper.

She looked away from him uncertainly. "I don't know. She went right up to her room."

Ethan thrust the bottle back into his pocket. "Don't worry. I'll come down and mend it in the night," he said.

Ethan looked around the kitchen. He saw the same scene of shining comfort as he had last night.

The table had been carefully set and a clear fire glowed in the stove. The cat dozed by the stove, and Mattie carried a plate of doughnuts.

She and Ethan looked at each other in silence. Then she said the same thing she had said the night before. "I guess it's about time for supper."

7 Zeena's Plan

Ethan called upstairs. Zeena did not answer, so he went up and opened her door. The room was almost dark, but he could see her sitting by the window.

"Well, Zeena," he said. "Supper's about ready. Aren't you coming?"

She replied, "I don't feel as if I could touch a morsel." Then she turned her head toward him, "I'm a great deal sicker than you think," she said.

She continued to look at him, as if she had been singled out for a great fate. She said, "I've got complications."

Ethan knew that word was very important. Almost everyone in town had "troubles," but only a few had "complications." People could struggle for years against "troubles." They almost always died of "complications." Ethan had a feeling this was going to cost him a lot.

"What do you know about this doctor, anyway?" asked Ethan. "Nobody ever told you that before."

"I didn't need to have anybody tell me I was losing ground every day," she whined. "Everybody but you could see it. And everybody knows what a good doctor Dr. Buck is. He wants me to have a hired girl. He says I shouldn't do a single thing around the house."

"A hired girl?" Ethan asked.

"Yes. And Aunt Martha found me one right away. She'll be over tomorrow afternoon."

Anger was the first thing that occurred to Ethan. He knew that Zeena's doctor visit would cost him money. But he simply could not afford to hire any help.

"Did Dr. Buck tell you how I was supposed to pay her?" he asked, furious.

"No, he didn't."

"You know I haven't got the money to pay for a girl, Zeena. You're just going to have to send her back."

Then Zeena spoke in a level voice. "I thought you were to get 50 dollars from Andrew Hale for that lumber."

"Andrew Hale never pays under three months." He suddenly remembered the excuse he made for not driving Zeena to the station. Ethan was not good at telling lies. He had no practice in it. "I guess that was a misunderstanding," he went on.

"You don't have the money?"

"No," he said.

For a while she sat still. Then she said mildly, "Oh, I guess we'll make out."

"Of course we will! There's a whole lot more I can do for you, and Mattie—"

Zeena did not seem to be paying attention. "At least we won't have to pay for Mattie's board anymore."

"Not pay for Mattie's board—?" Ethan began.

Zeena laughed. It was an odd sound. Ethan didn't remember ever having heard her laugh before. "You didn't suppose I was going to keep two girls, did you? No wonder you were scared of the cost!"

"I don't know what you mean," he said. "Mattie Silver's not a hired girl. She's your relation."

"She's a pauper who's hung onto us after her father almost ruined us. I've kept her here for a whole year. It's somebody else's turn now."

As Zeena spoke, Ethan heard a tap on the door.

"Ethan—Zeena!" Mattie's cheerful voice came from the landing. "Do you know what time it is? Supper's been ready half an hour."

Zeena answered, "I'm not coming down to supper."

Ethan opened the door and spoke to Mattie. "Go along down, Matt. Zeena's tired. I'll be right down."

He heard her say, "All right!" Then he shut the door again and turned back to Zeena. His wife's attitude was unchanged, and her face was set. He was overcome with a sense of despair and helplessness.

"You're not going to do it, Zeena?"

"Do what?" she said, through flattened lips.

"Send Mattie away—like this?"

"I never agreed to take her for life!"

He continued, with rising anger, "You can't put her out of the house like a thief. She's a poor girl without friends or money. Everyone knows she's your kin. If you do this, what do you think folks will say of you?"

Zeena waited a moment, as if to show the contrast between his anger and her calm. Then she answered in a smooth voice. "I know what they say about my keeping her here as long as I have."

Ethan's hand dropped from the doorknob, which he'd held since he'd shut the door. Zeena's words showed him that it was useless to argue with her.

"You mean to tell her she's got to go—at once?"

As if trying to make him see reason, Zeena said, "Yes. The girl will be here tomorrow. She'll need somewhere to sleep."

Ethan looked at her with hatred. She was no longer the same person who had lived with him all these years. Now she seemed to be completely evil. Mattie was Zeena's relation, not his. There was no way he could force Zeena to keep the girl under their roof. All the long misery of his past rose up in his soul. It seemed to take shape before him in the woman who at every turn had barred his way.

She had taken everything else from him. Now she meant to take the one thing that had made up for all the others. For a moment such a flame of hate rose in him that it ran down his arm. He clenched his fist and took a wild step forward. Then he stopped.

"You're—you're not coming down?" he said in a confused voice.

"No. I guess I'll lie down a little while," she answered.

In the kitchen Mattie was sitting by the stove. The cat was curled up on her knees. She sprang to her feet as Ethan entered. Then she carried the covered dish of meat pie to the table.

"I hope Zeena isn't sick?" she asked.

"No."

She shone at him across the table. "Well, sit right down then. You must be starving." She uncovered the pie and pushed it over to him. So they were to have one more evening together, her happy eyes seemed to say!

He tried to eat, but he couldn't. He laid down his fork. Mattie watched him do this.

"Why, Ethan, what's the matter? Isn't it good?"

"Yes, it's first-rate. Only I—" he pushed the plate away and rose from his chair. He walked around the table to her side. She looked at him with frightened eyes.

"Ethan, something's wrong! I knew there was!"

She seemed to melt against him in her terror. He caught her in his arms and held her. He felt her lashes beat his cheek like butterflies in a net.

"What is it—what is it?" she stammered. But Ethan had found her lips and was kissing them. He was unaware of everything but the joy they gave him.

She was caught in the same emotions. Then she slipped away and drew back a step or two. She was pale and troubled. Her look hurt him, and he cried out, "You can't go, Matt! I'll never let you!"

"Go—go?" she stammered. "Must I go?"

Ethan was ashamed of his lack of control in telling her the news so suddenly. He felt dizzy and he had to support himself against the table. He felt as if he were still kissing her, and yet dying of thirst for her lips.

"Ethan, what has happened? Is Zeena angry?"

"No, no," he said. "It's not that. But this new doctor says she won't get well unless she lies in bed. He says she is not to work around the house."

He stopped talking, his eyes looking away in misery. She stood silent, drooping like a broken branch. She was so small and weak-looking that it hurt Ethan's heart. Then she lifted her head and looked straight at him. "And she wants a better housekeeper in my place? Is that it?"

"That's what she says." They both knew that Zeena never changed her mind. Once she decided something, it was as good as done.

There was a long silence between them. Then Mattie said in a low voice, "Don't be too sorry, Ethan."

"Oh, God—oh, God," he groaned. The glow of passion he had felt for her had become an aching tenderness. He saw her quick lids beating back the tears. He longed to take her in his arms and soothe her.

"You're letting your supper get cold," she said.

"Oh, Matt—Matt—where will you go?"

Her lids sank and her face trembled. "I might get something to do over at Stamford." She said it as if she knew she had no hope.

He dropped back into his seat and hid his face in his hands. What chance did she have among all the other job-seekers? She had no experience and no training. He thought of all the terrible stories he'd heard about what happened to girls like Mattie. He could not think of such things without feeling sick.

"You can't go, Matt! I won't let you! She's always had her way, but I mean to have mine now—"

Suddenly Ethan heard his wife's step behind him. "I feel a little better. Dr. Buck says I ought to eat all I can to keep my strength up," she whined. She reached for the teapot, poured out her tea, and added a great deal of milk to it. Then she helped herself to pie and pickles. As usual, she adjusted her false teeth before she began to eat.

Ethan could not eat, but Mattie nibbled at her food. She asked Zeena one or two questions about her trip. Zeena answered in her normal tone of voice. She looked straight at Mattie as she spoke. A faint smile deepened the lines between her nose and chin.

When supper was over she pressed her hand near her heart. "That pie of yours always sets a little heavy, Matt," she said. "I think I'll try some of those stomach powders I got last year. Maybe they'll help the heartburn."

Mattie said, "Can't I get them for you, Zeena?"

"No. They're in a place you don't know about," Zeena answered. She went out of the kitchen. Mattie began to clear the table. As she passed Ethan's chair, their eyes met and clung together.

Moments later, Zeena came back into the room, her lips twitching in anger. In her hands she carried the pieces of the red glass pickle dish.

"I'd like to know who did this," she said.

There was no answer. Zeena continued, "I went to get those powders that I'd put on top of the china closet—" Her voice broke, and two small tears hung on her lashless lids and ran down her cheeks. "I put the pickle dish up there on purpose. I didn't want it to get broken." She laid the pieces solemnly on the table. "I want to know who did this."

Ethan faced her. "I can tell you, then, Zeena. The cat did it."

"The cat?"

"That's what I said."

Zeena turned her eyes toward Mattie. "I'd like to know how the cat got into my china closet."

"Chasing mice, I guess," said Ethan.

Zeena looked from one to the other and then said, "I knew the cat was a smart cat. I just didn't know he was smart enough to pick up the pieces of my pickle dish. Not only that, he put them back where they came from."

Mattie suddenly said, "It wasn't Ethan's fault, Zeena! The cat did break the dish. But I got it down from the china closet. I'm the one to blame for its getting broken."

Zeena stiffened. "You got down my pickle dish? What for?"

A bright flush flew to Mattie's cheeks. "I wanted to make the supper table pretty."

"So you waited till my back was turned and took my favorite dish. I wouldn't even use it, not even when the minister came to dinner." Zeena stopped with a gasp. "You're a bad girl, Mattie Silver, and I always knew it. You're just like your father. I was warned of it when I took you. I tried to keep my things where you couldn't get at them. And now you've broken the one thing I cared for most of all—" Zeena broke off, sobbing.

"If I would have listened to folks, you'd have been gone long ago," Zeena went on. "This would never have happened." Then she gathered up the bits of broken glass. She went out of the room as if she carried a dead body. . . .

8 Ethan's Last Hope

Years before, Ethan had been called back to the farm by his father's illness. His mother had given him a small room downstairs. He had fixed the room up like a study. As soon as the house was quiet, he went to this room. He knew that Zeena was sound asleep.

After Zeena had gone upstairs, Mattie had finished clearing up the kitchen for the night. Ethan had gone on his usual check of the outside of the house. The kitchen was empty when he came back inside. His pipe and tobacco had been put on the table. Under them was a note that said, "Don't trouble, Ethan."

In his study, he read the message again and again. Holding the paper gave him a strange new sense of her nearness.

Confused emotions stormed inside him. He was too young, too strong, too full of life to give up his hopes so easily. Must he wear out all his years at the side of a bitter, whining woman? She was a hundred times worse than when he had married her. Her greatest pleasure seemed to be in causing him pain.

He knew about a man who had escaped from just such a life of misery. This man had gone West with the girl he cared for. His wife had divorced him, and he had married the girl and done well. The deserted wife had not done badly either. Her husband had given her the farm and she had sold it. With the money she opened a successful lunch room at Bettsbridge.

Ethan was fired by the thought. Why shouldn't he leave with Mattie the next day? He would hide his suitcase under the seat of the sleigh. Later, Zeena would find a letter on the bed.

He found a sheet of paper and began to write.

"Zeena, I've done all I could for you. I don't see that it's been any use. I don't blame you, nor do I blame myself. I'm going to try my luck living Out West. You can sell the farm and mill, and keep the money. . . ."

He stopped and thought about what this meant. If he gave everything to Zeena, what would be left for him? And what about Zeena? The farm and mill were not paid for. Even if she found a buyer, she would only clear about a thousand dollars. Meanwhile, how could she keep the farm going?

He had thrown the contents of the drawer around in his search for a sheet of paper. As he thought, his eye fell on an old copy of the Bettsbridge *Eagle*.

He read the words of an advertisement: "Trips to the West—Reduced Rates."

He drew the lantern nearer and read the rates. Then the paper fell from his hand, and he pushed the letter away. A moment ago he had wondered what he and Mattie would live on in the West. Now he saw that he didn't even have the money to take her there. Borrowing was out of the question. He knew that no one in Starkfield would lend him ten dollars. The facts closed in on him like handcuffs on a convict. There was no way out—none. He was a prisoner for life.

Tears rose in his throat. They slowly burned their way to his lids.

He looked through the window at the moon. This was the night he and Mattie were to have gone coasting. There was the moon, ready to light their way! It seemed that all the beauty of the night was there to mock his misery.

He fell asleep. When he woke, the chill of the winter dawn was in the room. He felt cold and stiff and hungry. He rubbed his eyes and went to the window. A red sun stood over the fields. He said to himself, "This is Matt's last day."

As he stood there, he heard a step behind him and she entered.

"Oh, Ethan—were you here all night? You must be frozen."

He stepped closer to her. "How did you know I was here?"

"I heard you go downstairs again after I went to bed. I listened all night, and you didn't come up."

All his tenderness rushed to his lips. He said, "I'll come right along and make up the kitchen fire."

They went to the kitchen, and he started the fire. As the kitchen grew warmer, Ethan's dark thoughts melted away. He watched Mattie going about her work. It seemed impossible that she should ever stop being part of this scene. He said to himself that he had exaggerated what Zeena said. He thought that, with the return of daylight, she would be in a better mood.

He went up to Mattie and laid his hand on her arm. "I don't want you to trouble either," he said.

She whispered, "No, Ethan, I won't."

"I guess things will straighten out," he added.

He left her and went out to the barn. He saw Jotham Powell walking up the hill through the morning mist. This familiar sight made him feel comfortable.

As the two men were clearing out the stalls, Jotham rested on his pitchfork. He said, "Daniel Byrne is going into town at noon today. He can take Mattie's trunk. That will make it easier for me to take her over in the sleigh."

Ethan looked at him blankly, and Jotham continued talking. "Mrs. Frome said the new girl would be coming in at five. I'll take Mattie at that time, and she can take the six o'clock train to Stamford."

Ethan felt the blood pounding in his head. He had to wait a moment before he could speak. Finally he said, "Oh, I'm not so sure about Mattie's going."

"Is that so?" said Jotham, and they went on with their work.

When they went to the kitchen, the two women were already at breakfast. Zeena asked Jotham, "What time did you say Daniel Byrne will be here?"

The hired man glanced over at Ethan. "About noon," he said.

Zeena turned to Mattie. "That trunk of yours is too heavy for the sleigh. Daniel Byrne will take it into town," she said.

"I'm much obliged to you, Zeena," said Mattie.

Ethan finished his morning tasks. Then he said to Jotham, "I'm going to Starkfield. Tell them not to wait lunch for me."

Ethan's anger had broken out in him again. What he thought was impossible was really going to happen. He was to watch helplessly as Mattie was banished. He wondered what Mattie must think of him. He had very confused thoughts as he walked to the village. He had made up his mind to do something. He just did not know what it would be.

Suddenly he thought that Andrew Hale might advance him a small sum on the lumber. He would tell Hale that Zeena's poor health made it necessary to hire a servant. Hale would surely believe that, and Ethan would not lose his pride by asking. Anyway, how much did pride count against the passions Ethan was feeling?

The more he thought about this plan, the more hopeful it seemed. With 50 dollars in his pocket, nothing could keep him from Mattie.

The first thing he had to do was reach Starkfield

before Hale left for work. Ethan walked even faster. Then he saw the Hales' sleigh coming toward him. Hale's youngest boy was holding the reins, and Mrs. Hale sat at his side. Ethan waved to them to stop. Mrs. Hale leaned forward, her pink wrinkles twinkling with goodness.

"Mr. Hale? Why, yes, you'll find him at home." Looking kindly on Ethan, she added, "I heard about Zeena's visit to the doctor. I'm so sorry she's feeling bad again! I always tell Mr. Hale how lucky Zeena is to have you. I used to say the same thing about your mother. You've had an awful mean time, Ethan Frome."

She gave him a nod of sympathy and her son started to drive off. Ethan stood in the middle of the road and stared after the sleigh.

It was a long time since anyone had spoken to him so kindly. Most people didn't seem to care at all about Ethan's troubles. Now he felt less alone with his misery. If the Hales were sorry for him, they would surely help him. . . .

He started down the road toward their house, but then he stopped suddenly. For the first time, he saw what he was about to do. He was planning to take advantage of the Hales' sympathy by lying about why he needed money.

This way of looking at it caused Ethan to see his life as it was. He was a poor man, the husband of a sickly woman. If he deserted his wife, she would be alone and without any money. In order to desert her, he would have to deceive two kindly people. These people were the only ones who had felt sorry for him.

He turned and walked slowly back to the farm.

9 Mattie's Plan

At the kitchen door Daniel Byrne sat in his sleigh. Ethan went into the kitchen and found Zeena sitting there. "Where's Mattie?" he asked.

"I presume she's getting down her trunk."

"Alone?"

"Jotham Powell's down in the wood lot. Daniel Byrne says he can't leave that horse," replied Zeena.

Ethan ran up the stairs to Mattie's room. "Matt," he said in a low voice, but there was no answer. He put his hand on the doorknob and opened the door.

He saw Mattie sitting on the trunk in the middle of the floor. She was in her Sunday dress, her back turned toward the door. She had her face in her hands, and she was sobbing.

"Matt—oh, don't—oh, Matt!"

She lifted her wet face to his. "Ethan—I thought I wasn't ever going to see you again!"

"Not see me again? What do you mean?"

She sobbed, "Jotham said you wouldn't be here for lunch, and I thought—"

"You thought I wouldn't say good-bye?"

She clung to him without answering. He laid his lips on her hair, which had the fragrance of fresh sawdust in the sun. Through the door they could hear Zeena. "Daniel Byrne says you better hurry up if you want him to take that trunk."

Mattie dried her eyes and took hold of a handle of the trunk. Ethan said, "You let go, Matt." Then he picked up the trunk and carried it down the stairs. Zeena did not lift her head from the book she was reading. Mattie followed Ethan out of the door. She helped him to lift the trunk into the sleigh.

It seemed to Ethan that his heart was tied with rope and an unseen hand was tightening it. Twice he opened his lips to speak to Mattie and found no breath. Finally, he said, "I'm going to drive you over, Matt."

She replied, "I think Zeena wants me to go with Jotham."

"I'm going to drive you over," he repeated.

They went inside to have lunch. Ethan could not even eat. Zeena ate well, saying that the mild weather made her feel better. When the meal was over, Mattie cleared the table and washed the dishes. Jotham Powell got ready to leave. He asked Ethan, "What time should I come back for Mattie?"

Ethan answered, "You don't have to come. I'm going to drive her over myself."

He saw the rise of color in Mattie's cheek. He also

saw the quick lifting of Zeena's head.

"I want you to stay here this afternoon, Ethan," his wife said. "Jotham can drive Mattie over."

Ethan repeated, "I'm going to drive her over myself."

Zeena said, "I want you to fix that stove in Mattie's room before the girl gets here. It hasn't been drawing right for about a month now."

Ethan's voice rose with anger. "If it was good enough for Mattie, I guess it's good enough for a hired girl."

Zeena said, "That girl said that she's used to a house that's warm."

"She should have stayed there then," said Ethan. Then he said to Mattie, "Be ready by three."

Ethan went out to the barn to get the horse ready for the trip. He remembered doing the same thing just over a year ago, before he picked Mattie up. He climbed into the sleigh and drove up to the house. The kitchen was empty, but Mattie's things were by the door. He thought he heard someone moving about in his study. He opened the door and saw Mattie, standing with her back to him. She heard him come in and turned around. "Is it time?" she asked.

"What are you doing here, Matt?" he asked her.

"I was just taking a look around—that's all," she answered.

They went back to the kitchen, and Ethan asked, "Where's Zeena?"

"She went upstairs. She had those shooting pains again, and didn't want to be disturbed."

"Didn't she say good-bye to you?"

"No. That was all she said."

Ethan looked about the kitchen. He realized that in a few hours he would be returning to it alone. He could hardly believe this was happening.

"Come on," he said, opening the door and putting her bag into the sleigh. They got in, and he shook the reins.

"We have lots of time for a good ride, Matt!" he said. He took her hand in his. His face tingled and he felt dizzy. They drove slowly up the road between fields shining under the pale sun. The road passed into a pine woods with trees reddening in the afternoon sun. Blue shadows lay across the snow. As the breeze fell, a warm stillness seemed to drop from the branches.

Ethan drove in silence until he came to a clearing in the woods. He stopped and helped Mattie get out of the sleigh. They walked among the trees, the snow breaking crisply under their feet. They came to a small frozen pond. Ethan looked up and down the little beach until he saw a fallen tree trunk half hidden by snow.

"That's where we sat at the picnic," he said.

He was speaking of the church picnic of last summer. Mattie had begged him to go with her, but he had refused. Then, toward sunset, he was coming back from cutting down trees in the forest. He had been drawn into the group near the lake by some other picnickers.

There he saw Mattie surrounded by other happy young people. He remembered how her face had lit up when she saw him. She had broken away from the group to come to him. They had sat for a few minutes on the fallen log by the pond. She had lost her locket, and had sent the young men to find it. Ethan had spied it in the moss. That was all, but the whole afternoon was a very happy moment for Ethan.

They both sat down on the tree trunk. "It was right there I found your locket," he said.

"I never saw anybody with such sharp eyes!" she answered.

"You were as pretty as a picture in that pink hat," he said.

For a moment, Ethan felt as if he were a free man, out with the girl he meant to marry. He looked at her hair and longed to touch it again.

Suddenly she rose to her feet. She said, "We mustn't stay here any longer."

"There's plenty of time," he said.

They stood looking at each other for a moment, and then walked in silence to the sleigh. As they drove away, the sun sank behind the hill. The trees turned from red to gray.

They drove on, and Ethan said, "Matt, what will you do?"

"I'm not sure."

"Wouldn't any of your father's folks help you?"

"There isn't anyone I would ask," said Mattie.

He lowered his voice. "You know there's nothing I wouldn't do for you if I could."

"I know there isn't."

"But I can't—"

She turned to him, pulling a scrap of paper from her pocket. "Ethan—I found this," she said.

Even in the dim light he saw it was the letter to his wife that he'd written the night before. "Matt," he cried, "if I could have done it, would you?"

"Oh, Ethan, Ethan, what's the use?" She tore the letter into small pieces and sent them fluttering into the snow.

"Tell me, Matt! Tell me!" he demanded.

In a low voice she said, "I used to think of it on summer nights."

His heart reeled. "As long ago as that?"

She answered, as if the date were very important, "The first time was at the church picnic. When I saw you coming down the road, I was so happy. I thought you came that way on purpose."

"I'm tied hand and foot, Matt. There isn't a thing I can do," he said.

"You must write to me sometimes, Ethan."

"What good will writing do? I want to put my hand out and touch you. I want to be with you and care for you. I want to be there when you're sick and when you're lonesome. Now you'll probably marry someone else!"

"Oh, Ethan!" she cried.

"I don't know why I feel this way, Matt. I'd almost rather see you dead than married to someone else!"

"Oh, I wish I was, I wish I was," she sobbed.

He felt ashamed of himself. "Let's not talk this way," he whispered.

"Why not, when it's true? I've been wishing it every minute of the day. No one has ever been good to me but you."

"Don't say that, Matt, when I can't even help you!"

"It's true, Ethan."

They had reached the top of the hill that led into Starkfield. They saw some boys dragging sleds up the hill. "I guess that will be their last coast for today," Ethan said. "We were supposed to go coasting last night."

Suddenly Ethan had an idea. "How would you like to go coasting now?"

She forced a laugh. "Why, there isn't time!"

"There's all the time we want. Come along!" Ethan's one desire was to put off the moment when he would have to return home.

"But the girl," said Mattie. "She'll be waiting at the station."

"Well, let her wait," said Ethan. "You'd have to if she didn't. Come!"

"But there isn't a sled around anywhere," Mattie said.

"Yes, there is! Right there under the spruces." Ethan caught Mattie's hand and pulled her toward the sled. She sat down, and he took his place behind her. They were so close that her hair brushed his face.

She turned her head to say, "It's terribly dark. Are you sure you can see?"

He laughed, "I could go down this coast with my eyes closed!" She laughed with him. Even so, he sat still a moment. It was true that he could hardly see.

"Now!" he cried.

The sled started, and they flew down the hill. They gained speed as they went, with the air singing by like an organ. Mattie sat perfectly still, except when they reached the bend at the foot of the hill. There the big elm thrust out a deadly elbow. Ethan felt Mattie shrink a little closer to him.

"Don't be scared, Matt!" he cried. They spun

safely past the elm and flew down the second slope. When they reached the level ground, he heard her laugh.

They got off the sled and started to walk back up the hill. Ethan dragged the sled behind him. "Were you scared I'd run you into the elm?" he asked.

"I told you I was never scared with you," she answered.

Deep silence had fallen with the darkness. With every step Ethan said to himself, "It's the last time we'll ever walk together."

When they got to the top of the hill, he said, "This must be Ned Hale's sled. I'll leave it where I found it." He rested the sled against the fence. Suddenly he felt Mattie close to him among the shadows. She flung her arms around him. Her lips, looking for his, swept over his face. He held her tight in a rapture of surprise.

"Good-bye—good-bye, Ethan," she stammered, and kissed him again.

"Oh, Matt, I can't let you go!" he cried.

"Oh, I can't go either!" she wailed.

"Matt! What'll we do? What'll we do?"

They clung to each other's hands like children. Her body shook with sobs. Through the stillness they heard the church clock strike five.

"Oh, Ethan, it's time!" she cried.

"Time for what?" he said. "You don't suppose I'm going to leave you now?"

"If I missed my train, where would I go?"

"Where will you go if you catch it?"

She stood silent, her hands in his.

"What's the good of either of us going anywhere without the other one now?" he said.

Suddenly she threw her arms around his neck and pressed her cheek against his face. "Ethan! Ethan! I want you to take me down again!"

"Down where?"

"The hill. Right now. So we'll never come up again."

"Matt! What on earth do you mean?"

She put her lips against his ear. "Right into the big elm. So we'd never have to leave each other anymore."

"Why, what are you talking of? You're crazy!"

"I'm not crazy. But I will be if I leave you."

"Oh, Matt, Matt—" he groaned.

"Ethan, where will I go if I leave you? And there will be that strange girl in the house. She'll sleep in my bed, where I used to lie nights and listen to hear you come up the stairs."

Her words were like fragments torn from his heart. He thought of the house he was going back to. He thought of the woman who would wait for him there. And he thought of the sweetness of what

Mattie had said. Knowing that she felt the same way as he did made his other life seem even worse.

"Come," Mattie whispered, tugging at his hand.

He pulled the sled out. The slope below them was empty. All Starkfield was at supper. He took his seat on the sled and Mattie sat in front of him. Suddenly he sprang up again.

"Get up," he ordered her.

"No, no, no!" she said.

"Get up!"

"Why?"

"I want to sit in front."

"No, no! How can you steer in front?"

"I don't have to. We'll follow the track."

"Why do you want to sit in front?" she asked.

"Because I want to feel you holding me," he said, dragging her to her feet.

The answer seemed to satisfy her, and she did what he asked. She waited while he seated himself in the front of the sled. Then she got in behind him and put her arms around him. Her breath on his neck made him tremble again. She was right, he thought. This was better than parting. He leaned back and drew her mouth to his.

They started down the hill. Halfway down there was a sudden drop, then a rise, and after that another long drop. It seemed to him as if they were flying. Then the big elm shot up ahead, lying in wait

for them at the bend of the road. He said, "We can
do it. I know we can do it."

The big tree loomed bigger and closer. As they
got closer, he thought, "It's waiting for us. It seems
to know." But suddenly his wife's face, with its
twisted lines, seemed to appear before him. He

made a quick movement to brush it aside. The sled swerved the same way he moved, but he straightened it again. He kept the sled straight and drove down toward the tree. There was a last instant when the air shot past him like millions of fiery wires. Then the elm . . .

The sky was still dark, but looking up he saw a single star. He thought it might be Sirius, or—or— Thinking made him very tired, and he closed his lids and thought he would sleep. . . . He thought he heard a little animal twittering somewhere nearby under the snow. It made a small frightened cheep like a field mouse. He wondered if it were hurt. Then he understood that it must be in pain. The pain was so bad that he seemed to feel it shooting through his own body.

He tried to roll over toward the sound. Now it seemed that he felt rather than heard the twittering. It seemed to be under his palm, which rested on something soft and springy. The thought of the animal's suffering was unbearable to him. He continued to feel about with his hand. He thought he might get hold of the little creature and help it. All at once he knew that the soft thing he touched was Mattie's hair. His hand was on her face.

He dragged himself to his knees. His hand went over and over her face. He felt that the twittering came from her lips. . . .

He got his face down close to hers. He put his ear to her mouth. He saw her eyes open and heard her say his name.

"Oh, Matt, I thought we'd done it," he moaned. Far off, up the hill, he heard his horse whinny. He thought, "I ought to be getting him his feed. . . ."

Epilogue

The whining stopped as I entered Frome's kitchen. Of the two women sitting there, I could not tell which had been the speaker.

One of them raised her tall bony figure from her seat. She wore a sloppy house dress. Her thin gray hair had been put into a bun at the back of her head. Her pale eyes revealed nothing. Her narrow lips were the same pale color as her face.

The other woman was much smaller and slighter. She sat in an armchair by the stove. When I came in, she turned her head toward me, but her body did not move. Her hair was as gray as the other woman's, and her face was as pale. Under her shapeless dress her body was limp and motionless. Her dark eyes had the bright stare that disease of the spine sometimes gives.

"My, it's cold here! The fire must be almost out," Frome said.

The tall woman did not answer. The other one said in a high, thin voice, "It's only been made this very minute. Zeena fell asleep and slept ever so long. I thought I'd be frozen stiff before I could wake her up to 'tend to it."

I knew then that it was this woman who had been speaking when we entered.

The other woman brought a cold mince pie to the table. Frome looked at me and said, "This is my wife, Mrs. Frome." After a moment, he turned toward the figure in the armchair. "And this is Miss Mattie Silver. . . ."

Mrs. Hale, tender soul, had thought I was lost in a snowstorm. She was very glad to see me the next morning. She and her mother were amazed to hear that Ethan Frome's old horse had made it through the worst blizzard of the winter. They were even more surprised to hear that Frome had taken me in for the night.

"Well," said Mrs. Hale, "I think you're the first stranger in that house for over 20 years. He's so proud that he doesn't even like his oldest friends to go there. I think the doctor and I are the only ones who go there anymore."

"You still go there, Mrs. Hale?" I asked.

"I used to go often after the accident, when I was first married. Then I started to think it made them feel worse to see us. And then one thing and another came, and my own troubles. I usually try to get out there twice a year—at New Year's and in the summer. I always try to pick a day when Ethan's not home. It's bad enough to see the two women sitting there. But his face, when he looks around that bare place, just kills me. You see, I can remember his face in his mother's day, before their troubles."

I said, "Yes, it's pretty bad, seeing all three of them there together."

She drew her brows into a frown of pain. "It was just awful from the beginning. I was here in the house when they were carried up. They laid Mattie Silver in the room you're in. She and I were great friends. She was going to be my bridesmaid in the spring. When she came to, I went up to her and stayed all night. They gave her things to quiet her. She didn't know much until morning. All of a sudden she woke up and looked straight at me, and said . . . Oh, I don't know why I'm telling you all this," Mrs. Hale broke off, crying.

She took off her glasses and wiped the tears from them. She went on, "News got around the next day that Zeena Frome had sent Mattie off in a hurry. There was a hired girl coming. Folks here could never figure out why she and Ethan were coasting that night. They were supposed to be on their way to catch the train. I never knew what Zeena thought. I still don't, to this day. Nobody knows Zeena's thoughts. Anyhow, when Zeena heard about the accident she came over and stayed with Ethan at the minister's. That's where they had carried him.

And as soon as the doctors said that Mattie could be moved, Zeena sent for her. She took her back to the farm."

"And there she's been ever since?"

Mrs. Hale answered simply, "There was nowhere else for her to go." My heart tightened at the thought of the hard lives of the poor.

"Yes, there she's been," Mrs. Hale continued. "Zeena's taken care of her and Ethan, as much as she could. It was a miracle, considering how sick she was. But she seemed to be raised right up just when the call came to her. Of course, she's had her own sick spells all along. But somehow she's had the strength to care for those two for more than 20 years. Before the accident she thought she couldn't even take care of herself."

Mrs. Hale paused for a moment. I murmured, "It's horrible for them all."

"Yes, it's pretty bad. And they're not easy people, either. Mattie was, before the accident. I never knew a sweeter nature. But she's suffered too much. That's what I always say when folks tell me how she's soured. And Zeena, she was always cranky. Sometimes the two of them get going at each other. When that happens, Ethan's face would break your heart. When I see that, I think it's Ethan that suffers most. It's certainly not Zeena—she doesn't have the time. The whole thing is a pity, though," Mrs. Hale ended, sighing. "They're all shut up there in that one kitchen. In the summer, they can move Mattie to the parlor or out into the yard. But in the winter, there's the fires to be thought of. There isn't a dime to spare up at the Fromes'."

Mrs. Hale took a deep breath. I thought she would say no more. Suddenly, she took off her glasses again and leaned toward me across the table. She lowered her voice, and said, "There was one day, about a week after the accident, when they all thought Mattie couldn't live. Well, I say it's a pity she did. I said it right out to the minister once, and he was shocked at me. But he wasn't with me that morning when she first came to. . . . I say, if she had died, Ethan might have lived. The way they are now, there's not much difference between the Fromes at the farm and the Fromes in the graveyard. There's only one small difference. In the graveyard they're all quiet, and the women have got to hold their tongues."

Golden Sierra High School
HL FIC Wha
Ethan Frome
7481

A PACEMAKER CLASSIC

S I M O N   &   S C H U S T E R

FEARON/JANUS/QUERCUS
500 Harbor Boulevard
Belmont, California 94002

ISBN 0-8224-9354